FOOD CHAINS

FOOD CHAINS AND YOU

Bobbie Kalman

🌱 Crabtree Publishing Company

www.crabtreebooks.com

Food Chains and You

Created by Bobbie Kalman
Dedicated by Andrea Crabtree
To Tom, thanks for making me laugh!

Author and Editor-in-Chief
Bobbie Kalman

Editors
Molly Aloian
Kristina Lundblad
Kelley MacAulay
Kathryn Smithyman

Art director
Robert MacGregor

Design
Katherine Berti

Pint and production coordinator
Katherine Berti

Photo research
Crystal Sikkens

Consultant
Patricia Loesche, Ph.D., Animal Behavior Program,
Department of Psychology, University of Washington

Photographs
Marc Crabtree: page 25
Bobbie Kalman: front cover (girl), title page (middle), 14 (bottom),
    19 (bottom), 21 (left), 24, 27, 30
Other images by Adobe Image Library, Comstock, Corbis, Corel,
Creatas, Digital Stock, Digtal Vision, and Photodisc

Illustrations
Barbara Bedell: pages 9 (rabbit, mouse, and bobcat), 10-11 (all
    except butterfly, goose, acorns, corn, daffodil, and 2 plants-page
    10 top left and right), 24 (shark and squid), 25 (owl, weasel, and
    mouse), 27 (ground)
Katherine Berti: pages 10-11 (acorns), 25 (chicken)
Margaret Amy Salter: series logo, pages 7, 9 (sun and sunflower),
    10-11 (butterfly), 24 (aquatic plants, shrimp, and fish),
    27 (earthworm and crab)
Bonna Rouse: pages 9 (plant), 10-11 (goose, 2 plants-page 10 top
    left and right, corn, and daffodil), 25 (corn), 31

Crabtree Publishing Company
www.crabtreebooks.com   1-800-387-7650

Copyright © **2012 CRABTREE PUBLISHING COMPANY.**
All rights reserved. No part of this publication may be reproduced,
stored in a retrieval system or be transmitted in any form or by
any means, electronic, mechanical, photocopying, recording, or
otherwise, without the prior written permission of Crabtree
Publishing Company. In Canada: We acknowledge the financial
support of the Government of Canada through the Canada Book
Fund for our publishing activities.

Printed in Canada/042013/MA20130325

The Library of Congress has cataloged the printed edition as follows:

Kalman, Bobbie.
    Food chains and you / Bobbie Kalman.
        p. cm. -- (Food chains series)
    Includes bibliographical references and index.
    ISBN 0-7787-1942-1 (RLB) -- ISBN 0-7787-1988-X (pbk.)
    1. Food chains (Ecology)--Juvenile literature. I. Title.
QH541.14.K3496 2005
577'.16--dc22
                                                                    2004014158
                                                                    LC

Published in Canada
Crabtree Publishing
616 Welland Ave.
St. Catharines, Ontario
L2M 5V6

Published in the United States
Crabtree Publishing
PMB 59051
350 Fifth Avenue, 59th Floor
New York, New York 10118

Published in the United Kingdom
Crabtree Publishing
Maritime House
Basin Road North, Hove
BN41 1WR

Published in Australia
Crabtree Publishing
3 Charles Street
Coburg North
VIC, 3058

Contents

Living things need food

People are living things. We share the Earth with plants and animals, which are also living things. Living things may not all look the same, but most of them need the same things to stay alive. They need air. They need water. They need sunlight, and they need food.

4

Nutrients and energy

Food contains **nutrients**. The nutrients in food give living things **energy**. Energy is the power living things need to stay alive. Living things need energy to grow, move, find food, and stay healthy. All living things get energy from food, but they do not all get their food in the same way.

Caterpillars and butterflies eat plants to get energy. Do you know how plants get energy?

Energy from the sun

All living things need energy. Energy flows from one living thing to another. As it flows, energy changes. Almost all energy begins with sunlight. Plants make food using sunlight. Only plants can change the sun's energy into food energy.

Food from sunlight

Plants **absorb**, or take in, the sun's energy and change it into food. The food that plants make is called **glucose**. Glucose is a type of sugar. It gives plants the energy they need to grow and to make new plants. Plants do not use all the food they make. They store some of it.

Chlorophyll magic

The leaves of plants contain **chlorophyll**. Chlorophyll is a green **pigment,** or color, that catches the sun's energy and uses it to make food.

Photosynthesis

Making food from sunlight is called **photosynthesis**. "Photosynthesis" comes from two words: "photo," which means "light," and "synthesis," which means "combination." Plants use sunlight to combine water and **carbon dioxide** to make food. Carbon dioxide is a gas that is found in air.

Plants clean the air

Too much carbon dioxide is harmful to animals and people. When plants use carbon dioxide to make food, they clean the air at the same time. As they make food, plants also let off **oxygen**. Animals and people need to breathe oxygen, which is also a gas found in air.

Plants use sunlight to make food.

During photosynthesis, the leaves of plants release oxygen into the air.

*The leaves of plants also release tiny droplets of water called **water vapor** into the air. Water vapor makes the air moist.*

Leaves take in carbon dioxide from the air.

The roots of plants take in water and nutrients from the soil. (See page 27.)

What is a food chain?

Plants **produce**, or make, their own food through photosynthesis. For this reason, they are called **producers**. Animals and people cannot make food using photosynthesis. They are called **consumers** because they must **consume**, or eat, other living things to get energy.

Energy flows

The sun's energy flows from plants to animals in **food chains**. When an animal eats a plant, it gets some of the sun's energy that was stored in the plant.

Energy from animals

Some animals do not eat plants. Instead, they eat other animals, but they still get the sun's energy. They get it by eating animals that have eaten plants. To see how a food chain works, look at the diagram on the right.

A food chain

These plants use the sun's energy to make food. They use some of the energy and store the rest.

When a rabbit eats sunflower seeds or dandelion leaves, some of the energy stored in those plants goes into the rabbit. The rabbit gets less of the sun's energy than the plants received.

When a bobcat eats the rabbit, only a little of the sun's energy is passed on to the bobcat through the plants and then through the rabbit.

An energy pyramid

As animals eat food, energy is passed from one living thing to another. The **energy pyramid** on the right shows this flow of energy. The pyramid is wide at the first level to show that there are many plants that make food energy. The pyramid narrows to show that there are fewer living things at the second level. Why do you think the pyramid is even narrower at the top level?

Third level: carnivores

The third level of a food chain is made up of **carnivores**. Carnivores are animals that get energy by eating other animals. Carnivores are the **secondary consumers** in a food chain. Secondary consumers eat primary consumers. They are at the top of the food chain, where there is much less energy. For this reason, there are fewer carnivores than there are herbivores or plants.

Second level: herbivores

The second level of a food chain is made up of **herbivores**. Herbivores are animals that eat mainly plants. Herbivores are the **primary consumers** in a food chain. Primary consumers are the first living things in a food chain that must eat to get energy. Herbivores must eat many plants to get the energy they need to survive. For this reason, there are fewer herbivores than there are plants.

First level: plants

The **primary**, or first, level of a food chain is made up of plants. Plants are called **primary producers** because they make food and are the first links in a food chain. There are more plants than there are animals. It takes many plants to feed all the animals in a food chain!

Animals that eat plants

Herbivores are animals that eat mainly plants. They eat different kinds of plants. Many eat grass, some eat flowering plants, and others eat parts of trees. All plants and plant parts contain some of the sun's stored energy.

Grazers and browsers

Herbivores that eat grass and small plants near the ground are **grazers**. Those that eat leaves, shoots, and twigs are **browsers**. Some of the biggest animals on Earth, such as elephants, rhinoceroses, and moose, are grazers or browsers.

Which plant parts?

Not all herbivores eat grass and leaves. Some insects and many birds drink **nectar**. Nectar is a sweet liquid found in flowers. Mice eat the seeds of plants. Other herbivores eat plant parts such as fruit, roots, and bark.

Squirrels eat seeds and nuts. They also eat fruits and other plant parts.

Plant foods for people

When you eat fruits and vegetables, you are eating plant foods. The sugars and **starches** stored in plants give your body nutrients called **carbohydrates**. Carbohydrates give you most of the energy you need. Plant foods also contain **fiber**. Fiber is a substance that is not digested by your body. You need fiber to help remove wastes from your body. Beans are a great source of fiber!

What are you eating?

Do you know which plant parts you are eating? Look at these plant foods and see if you can guess whether they are stems, roots, leaves, fruits, or seeds.

Most nuts are really hard-covered fruits, but peanuts are not nuts. They are seeds.

Celery stalks are stems. This picture also shows the leaves of the celery.

Is a tomato a fruit or a vegetable? If you guessed fruit, you were right!

Lettuce is made up of a bunch of leaves.

The dark spots around the center of the kiwi fruit are the seeds of the fruit.

When you eat broccoli, you are eating the flowers and stems of the broccoli plant.

*Bread is made from the seeds of grain plants such as wheat and rye. The **whole-grain bread** on the right contains more nutrients than does the white bread on the left.*

*Red and white potatoes are stems, but **yams**, or sweet potatoes, are roots. Other root vegetables are beets, carrots, and parsnips.*

Animals that hunt for food

Carnivores are meat-eaters. Most carnivores are **predators**. Predators hunt other animals for food. The animals they hunt are called **prey**. When they eat prey that are herbivores, they are secondary consumers.

When they eat other carnivores, they are **tertiary consumers**. The bobcat above is a secondary consumer when it eats mice and a tertiary consumer when it eats burrowing owls, which also eat mice.

Predators are important

Predators are important links in food chains. When there are no predators in an area, there are too many herbivores. The herbivores then eat most of the plants in that area.

When there are no wolves in an area, there can be too many deer. (See page 29.)

Healthy herds

Predators keep animal herds healthy because they often hunt sick and old animals. When sick and old animals are gone, there is more food for the healthy animals of the herd.

Lions and other big cats hunt the weak animals in a herd, such as this old zebra.

Eating the leftovers

Some animals do not hunt. They are called **scavengers** because they **scavenge**, or look for, dead animals that predators have left behind.

Hyenas and vultures are scavengers that eat what lions and other animals leave behind. Hyenas sometimes hunt as well as scavenge.

17

Animal foods for people

Meat comes from animals. Animals not only provide people with meat, but they also give us other foods such as milk and eggs. Dairy farmers raise cows for milk. Other farmers raise cows, pigs, chickens, or sheep for their meat. Fishers catch various fish such as salmon and trout for people to eat.

The cows in the picture above are eating grass. Energy from the sun is in the grass and now in the cows. When you eat beef, you also get the sun's energy in your body.

Full of nutrients

Animal products are rich in the nutrients your body needs, especially **protein**. Meat and milk products such as cheese and yogurt are protein-rich foods. Milk also contains a mineral called **calcium**. Protein and calcium give us strong bones, muscles, and teeth.

Yogurt is a milk product that tastes delicious. Many people like to mix fresh fruit such as bananas or berries into it!

19

Not fussy eaters

Many animals get their energy from either plants or animals, but some animals eat both. **Omnivores** eat both plants and other animals. Brown bears, for example, eat berries, insects, fish, and any other foods they find. Most omnivores have no trouble finding food because they are not fussy eaters.

Bears sleep through much of the winter. When they become active again in the spring, they are very hungry and go fishing for salmon. In summer, they feed on berries and other plant foods. If you are camping in an area where bears live, don't leave food where bears can reach it. They will steal your food!

Different seasons and foods

Skunks eat mainly insects, grubs, and small animals, but they also eat bird eggs and fruit. Animals that feed on any food they find are called **opportunistic feeders**. The foods they eat may change with the seasons or with the places in which the animals live.

These girls have cooked a great meal that contains meat, rice, beans, bread, and vegetables.

Are you an omnivore?

Just as omnivores eat several kinds of foods, people also eat different foods to get all the nutrients their bodies need. Most people eat both plant and animal foods. Which of the foods shown in this box come from plants, and which come from animals?

21

Where do we get food?

Cabbages grow in fields under the sun. When we eat fresh foods such as these, we get more of the sun's energy than when we eat canned or other processed foods.

In the past, people gathered berries from wild bushes and picked other fruits from trees that grew in nature. They hunted for meat and went fishing if they wanted to eat seafood.

Foods today

Today, we buy most of our food in supermarkets. It often comes wrapped in plastic or packaged in cardboard boxes. Many foods are **processed**. Processed foods have salt, sugar, and chemicals added to them, which may be harmful to people. All foods are part of food chains, but fresh foods contain more nutrients than do processed foods. They give us longer-lasting energy. Buying fresh foods is also better for the Earth. (See pages 30-31.)

(top left) Grains such as wheat, rye, and oats are grown in fields. They are ground into flour and used to make bread, noodles, and cereals.

(top right) Some fruits, such as pears, apples, and oranges, grow on trees.

(far right) Fruits and vegetables are picked by people and packed into boxes. They are then shipped to markets all over the world.

(right) Meat comes from animals such as lambs, pigs, cows, and chickens.

All the foods shown on these pages belong to food chains.

23

Food webs and you

Just as we eat different kinds of foods, most animals also belong to more than one food chain. When an animal from one food chain is eaten by an animal from another food chain, those animals are part of a **food web**. A food web includes many plants and animals, and there are many food webs. When you eat fish, you are part of a food web that contains a bear and another food web that includes a shark! You and many kinds of animals are part of different food webs.

An ocean food web

This diagram shows an example of a food web that includes you when you eat seafood. The arrows point toward the living things that receive the food energy.

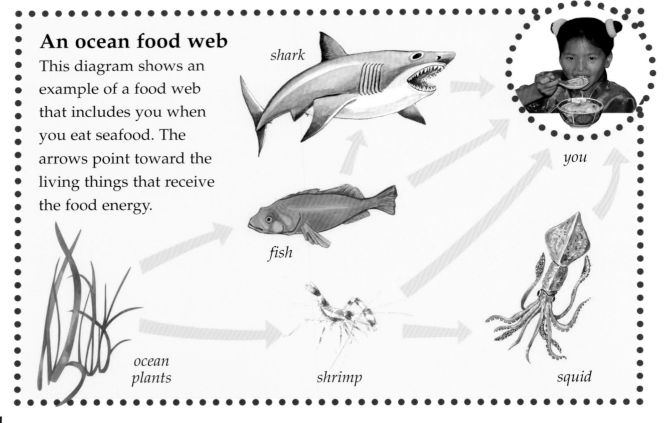

shark

you

fish

ocean plants

shrimp

squid

A food web on land

When you eat corn and chicken, you are part of a food web that includes an owl, a weasel, a mouse, as well as a chicken and some corn. Other animals in this food web might include a fox or a coyote. Both of these animals eat chickens and mice.

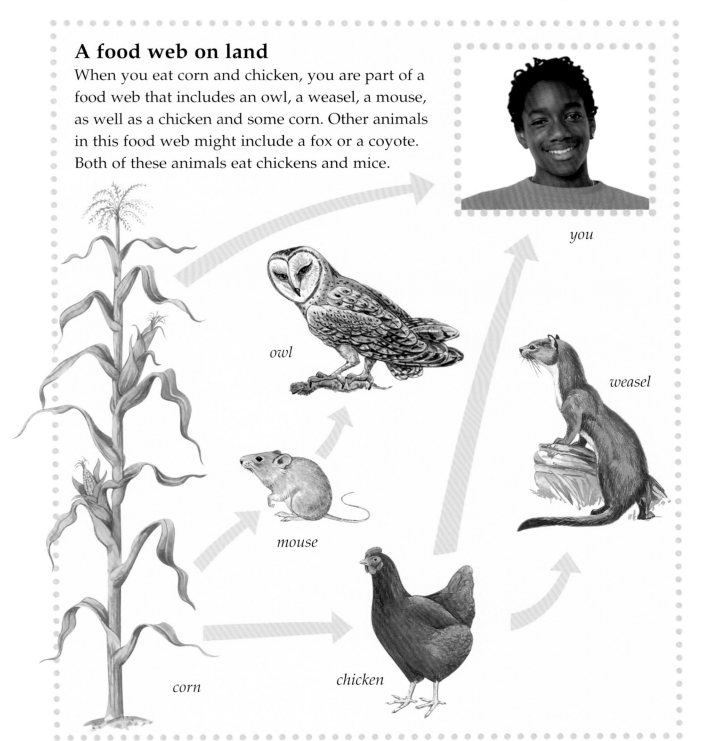

you

owl

weasel

mouse

corn

chicken

25

Nature's cleaners

On land, mushrooms, bacteria, and snails help break down dead plants and animals. In water, shrimps, clams, crabs, insects, and other decomposers break down dead things.

All living things die and become food for other living things called **decomposers**. Decomposers break down dead material so it can become part of the soil. If plants and animals died and were not broken down into smaller pieces, they would pile up. Soon, the Earth would be covered in dead things!

Detritus food webs

Bacteria, mushrooms, worms, slugs, and snails are all decomposers. They are part of **detritus food webs**. Detritus means decomposing material.

Reusing energy

Decomposers eat dead things to get the nutrients that are left inside them. They put the nutrients back into soil or water, where plants will grow. The plants then use these nutrients plus the energy of the sun to make food. Decomposers not only help plants grow, they also help keep the Earth clean for other living things.

What's really in your sandwich?

If you eat a grilled chicken sandwich with mushrooms, tomatoes, and lettuce, you are eating plants, a herbivore, and a decomposer. Crab, clams, lobster, and shrimp are other decomposers you might dine on from time to time. But what is really in your sandwich? When you eat any food, you are getting some of the sun's energy. You are also getting nutrients that have come from dead plants and animals in the soil or on the ocean floor. So, your sandwich is part sunshine, part soil, part water, and part dead things. When you eat anything, you are really eating a part of everything!

Dangers to food webs

Pesticides are harmful to insects, birds, and people. The man above is wearing a special suit and mask because the pesticide he is spraying is dangerous to his health. In some places, people are starting to use safer ways to kill pests.

There are more people on Earth every year, and they need to eat. Sometimes we forget that animals need to eat, too. People damage food chains and webs when they change nature. When people cut down forests to build farms or homes, they destroy the homes and food supplies of animals. Cutting down forests destroys food webs.

Using pesticides

When people use chemicals called **pesticides** on their lawns or on farms to kill pest insects, they also kill helpful insects such as bees and butterflies. Many plants need these helpful insects to make seeds so new plants can grow.

Hunting carnivores

In the past, people hunted animals such as tigers and wolves because they were afraid that these carnivores would eat their farm animals. In the oceans, sharks are still being killed because people are afraid of them. If you look at the energy pyramid on pages 10-11, you will see that there are fewer carnivores than there are other animals in food chains and webs. Killing carnivores throws food chains and webs off balance because carnivores are a very important part of the energy pyramid.

Off balance

When all the wolves are killed in an area, the number of deer grows each year. The deer eat too many wild plants and strip bark off trees, which kills the trees. Deer also visit people's back yards and eat their plants.

How you can help

There are many ways you can help food chains. The first step is knowing that your actions will change the lives of plants and animals. The second is letting others know how they can help, too. Get your family, friends, and neighbors involved!

Eat foods that are grown **locally**, or near your home. These foods are fresh because they did not have to be shipped from far away. Ask your parents to buy **organic** foods that contain no pesticides. Perhaps your family can plant a vegetable garden!

What do you eat?

When you eat mainly foods such as vegetables, grains, and fruit, you are helping to keep yourself healthy, and you are also helping the Earth. It takes more land, more fuel, and more water to raise animals than it does to raise plants. You can still eat meat and fish, but eat less of these foods. Eating more vegetables and grains is better for both you and the Earth, so think greens and grains!

In your back yard

Ask your parents to plant **native plants** in your back yard. Native plants are plants that have grown naturally in an area for thousands of years. They need less water and do not need pesticides. Native plants will also attract butterflies and birds to your back yard. If you have bird feeders, buy natural seeds such as sunflower seeds and thistle seeds instead of mixed birdseed. Cats are predators. If you have a cat, make sure you keep it indoors when the birds are feeding!

Glossary

Note: Boldfaced words that are defined in the text may not appear in the glossary.

bacteria Tiny living things that help break down dead plants and animals

calcium A mineral found in milk products, soy, almonds, and many vegetables, which is essential for buiding strong bones and teeth

carbohydrate A substance produced by plants, which is a major source of energy for animals

organic Describing something that is grown naturally, without chemicals

pesticide A chemical made to kill insects

protein A substance needed for growth, which is found in foods such as meat and soy beans

starch A nutrient found in foods such as potatoes, corn, and rice

whole-grain bread Bread made from grains that have not had their nutritious parts removed

Index